Searchlight
BOOKS™

What
Are Energy
Sources?

Finding Out about

Wind

Energy

Matt Doeden

Lerner Publications Company
Minneapolis

Lerner Publications Company
A division of Lerner Publishing Group, Inc.
241 First Avenue North
Minneapolis, MN 55401 USA

For reading levels and more information, look up this title at www.lernerbooks.com.

Library of Congress Cataloging-in-Publication Data

Doeden, Matt, author.
    Finding out about wind energy / by Matt Doeden.
        pages   cm. — (Searchlight books. What are energy sources?)
    Includes index.
    ISBN 978-1-4677-3656-5 (lib. bdg. : alk. paper)
    ISBN 978-1-4677-4642-7 (eBook)
    1. Wind power—Juvenile literature. 2. Wind turbines—Juvenile literature. I. Title.
TJ820.D64 2015
333.9'2—dc23   2013041259

Manufactured in the United States of America
1 — BP — 7/15/14

Contents

Chapter 1

WHAT IS WIND ENERGY?

Imagine flying a kite on a breezy day. The kite sails high above you in the sky. It dips, climbs, and darts around. It tugs hard on the string. A strong enough gust could even tear the kite from the string altogether.

Wind energy makes a kite fly. How else can people use wind energy?

Every movement of the kite is a result of wind energy. The same energy that lifts the kite can be used to make electricity that powers your home.

A wind sock flaps in the breeze.

Where Does Wind Energy Come From?

The power of wind comes from kinetic energy. This is the energy all moving objects have. The faster something is moving, the more kinetic energy it has. So a howling wind has a lot more energy than a gentle breeze.

You have kinetic energy when you run.

**Did you know that the
sun causes wind to blow?**

Wind is really just moving air. So where does the air
get all this kinetic energy? It comes from the sun.

Air over land heats up faster than air over water.

The sun's rays warm the air as they beat down on Earth. But some parts of the world heat up more than others. Hot air is lighter than cold air. The warmer air rises. Then heavier cold air rushes in to take its place. That's wind!

Where Do We Find Wind Energy?

We can find wind energy almost anywhere. That's because wind blows all around the world. But the best places to find wind energy are where the wind almost always blows. These places include flat coastal areas. There, strong winds come off the ocean.

Coastlines are good for making wind power because strong winds come off the ocean.

Flat, open plains are another spot with lots of wind energy. There's little to stop the wind as it races over open plains.

Chapter 2

COLLECTING WIND ENERGY

People have been collecting wind energy for thousands of years. The ancient Egyptians used wind power to move sailboats along the Nile River. This was about five thousand years ago or even earlier.

People have used wind energy since ancient times. How did the ancient Egyptians use it?

This photo shows early windmills.

Later, people in China and other parts of the world began building windmills. The wind spun the blades on the windmills. The spinning blades powered tools such as millstones. These large stones milled, or crushed, grain.

Windmills remained a way to collect wind energy into the twentieth century. Some still exist. But these days, we have a more efficient tool for collecting energy from wind.

This old-fashioned windmill is still in use.

The Wind Turbine

The turbine is the tool we use today to collect wind energy. Turbines can produce electricity from wind.

There are two main types of wind turbines. They

are called horizontal-axis turbines and vertical-axis turbines. Horizontal-axis turbines are the most common. They look a little like old-fashioned windmills. Blades are attached to a shaft that spins horizontally. The blades spin vertically. These turbines can be very large. The biggest ones stand 400 feet (122 meters) or taller.

These are horizontal-axis turbines.

This is a vertical-axis turbine.

Vertical-axis turbines have shafts that stand vertical to the ground. The blades spin around the shafts. The spinning blades look a little like an eggbeater.

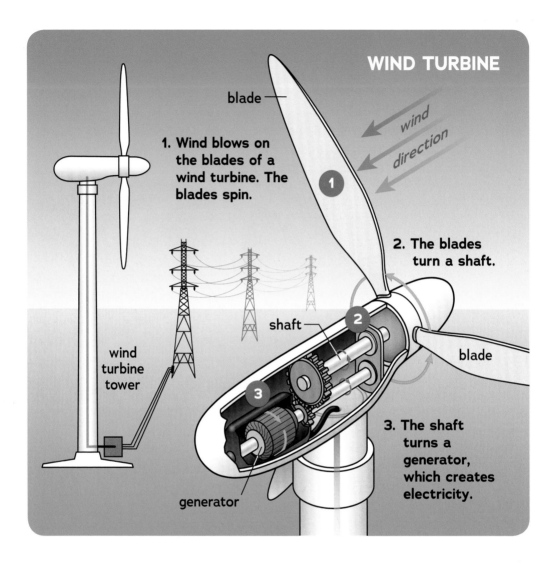

WIND TURBINE

blade

1. Wind blows on the blades of a wind turbine. The blades spin.

wind direction

2. The blades turn a shaft.

wind turbine tower

shaft

blade

3. The shaft turns a generator, which creates electricity.

generator

The idea behind both designs is the same. The wind pushes on the blades. The blades spin. The spinning blades turn a shaft. The shaft is connected to a generator. This machine turns the energy into electricity.

The Wind Farm

A single wind turbine can provide enough electricity for 350 homes or more. That's a lot. But it's not enough to make much of a dent in a city's energy needs. That's why we build wind farms.

Turbines spin on a wind farm near the mountains.

Wind farms are wind power plants that have a few to more than one hundred wind turbines. Wind farms work best in the windiest places.

Some wind farms, such as this one, are large. Others might have only a couple of turbines.

Offshore turbines, such as this one, are becoming more common.

In recent years, more wind farms have been placed offshore. These wind farms are in shallow coastal waters. There, they get stronger and more dependable winds. And they don't take up valuable land.

This wind farm is used to bring electricity to buildings.

Wind farms send the power straight into the power grid. The grid delivers the power to homes, businesses, and other places that need electricity.

Small Wind Systems

Not all wind power comes from huge wind farms. More and more people are setting up single small turbines.

These turbines can be as small as 7 feet (2.1 m) across. These turbines may produce only enough electricity to power a single home. Small systems are especially useful for rural areas that are not connected to the power grid.

You can get your own wind turbine to power your house!

Small wind turbines are often used in hybrid electric systems. In these, small wind turbines provide energy to a home or a business alongside other energy sources. These include solar power and fossil fuels.

Chapter 3

THE PROS AND CONS OF WIND ENERGY

Most of the world's energy comes from nonrenewable sources. These include fossil fuels such as coal, oil, and natural gas. Once we use a nonrenewable resource, it's gone forever.

This coal is a nonrenewable energy source. What are other nonrenewable sources of energy?

But wind is a renewable resource. As long as the sun shines, wind will continue to blow. Yet wind isn't a perfect energy source. It has many good points. But it also has some drawbacks.

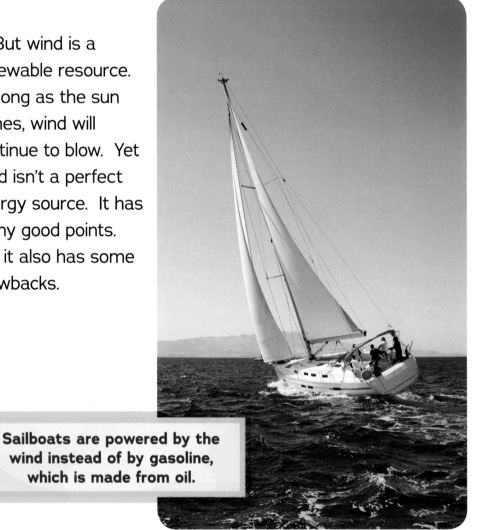

Sailboats are powered by the wind instead of by gasoline, which is made from oil.

The Environment

Wind is one of the cleanest ways to produce electricity. We can get electricity from wind without putting any pollution into the air. Burning fossil fuels gives off a lot of carbon dioxide.

Coal-burning power plants pollute the air.

Global climate change may cause more severe droughts.

Most scientists agree that this gas is causing Earth to warm. Too much warming could be a disaster. Wind turbines don't release any carbon dioxide. That makes them a great way to help slow global climate change.

Trouble for Wildlife

Wind farms can be a danger to wildlife. Wind farms have sprung up in birds' and bats' habitats. Each year, some of these animals are killed when they fly into wind turbines.

Birds and bats can be killed if they fly into a wind turbine's spinning blades.

Whooping cranes are sometimes hurt by wind turbines.

Some see wind farms as a big threat to endangered species, such as the whooping crane. But people continue to work toward reducing the number of bird and bat deaths. Better turbine design and placement is helping.

Trouble for People

People can also be bothered by wind farms. Some who live near wind farms say the turbines ruin the land's natural beauty.

Visual pollution is a term for when a man-made object interferes with a scenic view.

Some wind turbines can be noisy when their blades spin quickly.

Another problem is noise. Spinning turbines can be loud. People living nearby have claimed to suffer from headaches and trouble sleeping. But there is little evidence that links these issues to wind turbines.

Limits to Wind Power

Wind can produce a lot of power. But it is limited. Wind farms can't be built just anywhere. Really hilly or bumpy areas aren't very good for wind energy.

Rocky land is not ideal for building wind turbines.

Most wind turbines need the wind to be blowing at least 8 miles (13 kilometers) per hour to work. The turbines don't make any electricity if the wind isn't strong enough. That makes wind power unreliable.

Sometimes the wind doesn't blow. Turbines won't work on these days.

And wind that is too strong is also a problem. Wind turbines cannot operate safely in winds of more than 55 miles (89 km) per hour. So they can't even produce power during a windstorm.

Wind turbines cannot operate during hurricanes.

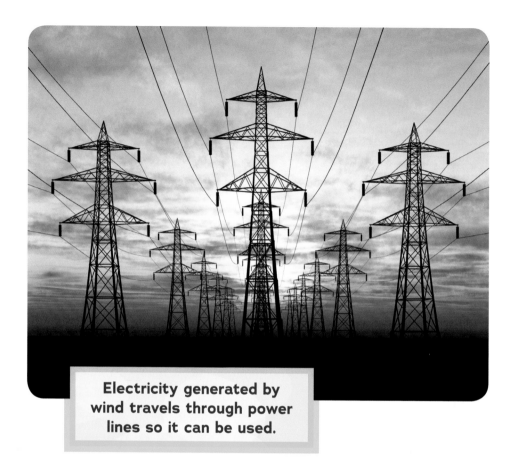

Electricity generated by wind travels through power lines so it can be used.

Another problem with wind power is storage. New ways of storing it are being developed. One way it can be stored is by using it to charge batteries for later use. But most times, it is used right away or wasted.

Chapter 4

WIND ENERGY IN THE FUTURE

Wind power is a growing part of the world's energy picture. Wind turbines in the United States can make enough electricity to power more than 15 million homes. And more wind farms are springing up every year.

Turbines stand tall behind these houses. How many homes in the United States can be powered by turbines?

Looking Ahead

We cannot depend on fossil fuels to provide most of the world's power forever. They will one day become too rare and too expensive to collect. That's why alternative energy sources are so important.

Digging up fossil fuels can damage the landscape. Burning them pollutes the air.

Wind energy may be a key part of the world's energy solution. Wind power is clean, plentiful, and renewable. It does have its limits, however. That's why it's only a piece of the puzzle. It must work alongside other energy sources. These include solar power and hydropower. Together, these and other energy sources may provide the world with all the power it needs.

Solar panels such as these can work alongside turbines to provide clean energy.

Glossary

alternative energy source: a source of energy other than traditional fossil fuels

endangered species: a type of living thing that is at risk of going extinct

fossil fuel: a fuel such as coal, natural gas, or oil that was formed over millions of years from the remains of dead plants and animals

generator: a machine that turns mechanical energy into electricity

hybrid: containing elements from two or more things

kinetic energy: the energy associated with a moving object

nonrenewable: not able to be replenished. Once a nonrenewable form of energy is gone, it is used up for good.

power grid: a system through which electricity is carried to homes and businesses

renewable: able to be replenished over time

turbine: a machine with blades that converts the energy from a moving fluid or gas, such as wind, into mechanical energy

unreliable: offering performance that is inconsistent and undependable

LERNER
SOURCE

Expand learning beyond the printed book. Download free, complementary educational resources for this book from our website, www.lerneresource.com.

Learn More about Wind Energy

Books

Boyle, Jordan. *Examining Wind Energy.* Minneapolis: Clara House Books, 2013. Read more about wind turbines, how they work, and the future of wind energy.

Doeden, Matt. *Finding Out about Coal, Oil, and Natural Gas.* Minneapolis: Lerner Publications, 2015. Fossil fuels remain our main source of energy. Learn more about how they form, how they're collected, and the pros and cons of using them.

Goodman, Polly. *Understanding Wind Power.* New York: Gareth Stevens, 2011. Learn more about the past, present, and future of wind power in this book.

Websites

Alliant Energy Kids—Wind Power
http://www.alliantenergykids.com/EnergyandTheEnvironment
/RenewableEnergy/022397
Pictures, text, and a diagram help kids better understand wind turbines and wind farms.

Energy Kids—Wind
http://www.eia.gov/kids/energy.cfm?page=wind_home-basics
This website gives a brief overview of wind and how and where we use it to produce electricity.

How Wind Power Works
http://science.howstuffworks.com/environmental/green-science
/wind-power.htm
This article is packed with information about wind and wind energy, including the uses of wind throughout history and modern-day wind farms.

Index

Photo Acknowledgments

The images in this book are used with the permission of: © iStockphoto.com/avdeev007, p. 4; © iStockphoto.com/Lightguard, p. 5; © iStockphoto.com/Squaredpixels, p. 6; © Ccaetano/Dreamstime.com, p. 7; © iStockphoto.com/Evgeny Kuklev, p. 8; © iStockphoto.com/TT, p. 9; © Dbrus/Dreamstime.com, p. 10; © The Bridgeman Art Library, p. 11; © Alireza Firouzi/Flickr Vision/Getty Images, p. 12; Warren Gretz/Department of Energy/National Renewable Energy Laboratory, p. 13; © iStockphoto.com/Volker Kreinacke, p. 14; © iStockphoto.com/BanksPhotos, p. 15; © Laura Westlund/Independent Picture Service, p. 16; © Photodisc/Getty Images, p. 17; Iberdrola Renewables, Inc./Department of Energy/National Renewable Energy Laboratory, p. 18; BARD Holding GmbH/Department of Energy/National Renewable Energy Laboratory, p. 19; © iStockphoto.com/dszc, p. 20; Bergey Windpower Co., Inc./Department of Energy/National Renewable Energy Laboratory, p. 21; © Creativenature1/Dreamstime.com, p. 22; © Pancaketom/Dreamstime.com, p. 23; © iStockphoto.com/travenian, p. 24; © iStockphoto.com/acilo, p. 25; © iStockphoto.com/Drbouz, p. 26; © J. Marijs/Shutterstock.com, p. 27; John Noll/USDA, p. 28; © iStockphoto.com/photovideostock, p. 29; © iStockphoto.com/archives, p. 30; © iStockphoto.com/jonmullen, p. 31; © iStockphoto.com/zxcynosure, p. 32; © iStockphoto.com/THEPALMER, p. 33; © iStockphoto.com/TebNad, p. 34; © iStockphoto.com/orhch, p. 35; © Venelin Petkov/Dreamstime.com, p. 36; © iStockphoto.com/prognone, p. 37.

Front cover: © iStockphoto.com/sharply_done.

Main body text set in Adrianna Regular 14/20
Typeface provided by Chank